ALFRED's
RED PERFORMER
COLLECTIONS

Gaither Gosp

MW00396151

Contemporary Settings of Cherished Songs Written by
Bill and Gloria Gaither

Arranged by Carol Tornquist

For generations, traditional hymnals have provided invaluable musical expressions of the Christian faith, and only songs that have stood the test of time have been included. However, hymnals in today's churches feature more than just traditional hymns; the gospel music genre is also well represented. Many songs in this genre were penned by Bill and Gloria Gaither and already qualify as classics. Their songs have been featured on the popular *Gaither Homecoming* television specials and on their website, www.gaither.com, making contemporary gospel music available to a wide audience.

On a personal note, I began my career in the Christian music business by arranging Gaither songs for solo piano, so revisiting them has been like becoming reacquainted with old friends. Although I have not taken these melodies too far from their musical roots, I have definitely arranged them in a contemporary style, which I hope will capture your musical imagination.

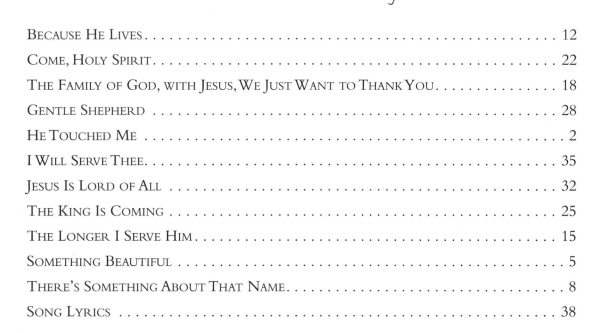

BECAUSE HE LIVES 12

COME, HOLY SPIRIT 22

THE FAMILY OF GOD, with JESUS, WE JUST WANT TO THANK YOU 18

GENTLE SHEPHERD 28

HE TOUCHED ME 2

I WILL SERVE THEE 35

JESUS IS LORD OF ALL 32

THE KING IS COMING 25

THE LONGER I SERVE HIM 15

SOMETHING BEAUTIFUL 5

THERE'S SOMETHING ABOUT THAT NAME 8

SONG LYRICS 38

Alfred

Produced by
Alfred Music Publishing Co., Inc.
P.O. Box 10003
Van Nuys, CA 91410-0003
alfred.com

Printed in USA.

ISBN-10: 0-7390-7648-5
ISBN-13: 978-0-7390-7648-4

Cover photo: © Nancy Bailey-Pratt

(Approx. Performance Time – 2:30)

HE TOUCHED ME

Words and Music by William J. Gaither
Arr. Carol Tornquist

Slowly, in two (♩ = 54)

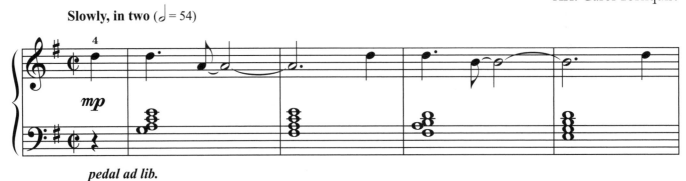

pedal ad lib.

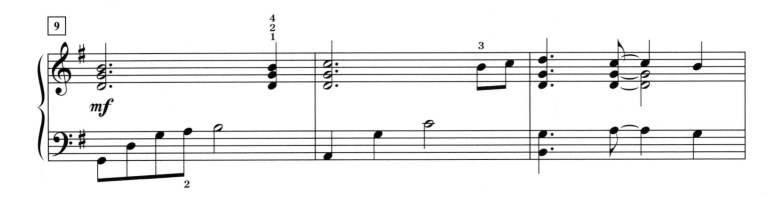

(Approx. Performance Time – 2:45)

Something Beautiful

Words by Gloria Gaither
Music by William J. Gaither
Arr. Carol Tornquist

(Approx. Performance Time – 3:00)

There's Something About That Name

Words by William J. and Gloria Gaither
Music by William J. Gaither
Arr. Carol Tornquist

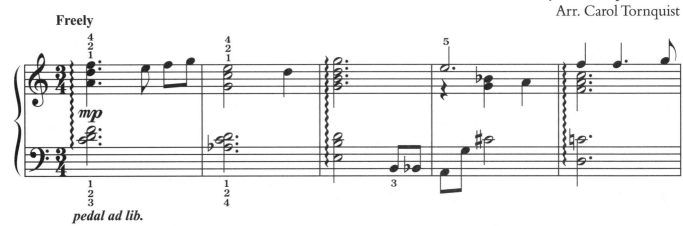

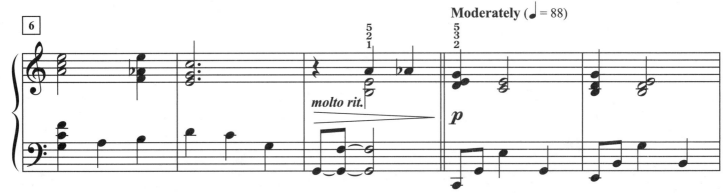

(Approx. Performance Time – 2:45)

BECAUSE HE LIVES

Words by William J. and Gloria Gaither
Music by William J. Gaither
Arr. Carol Tornquist

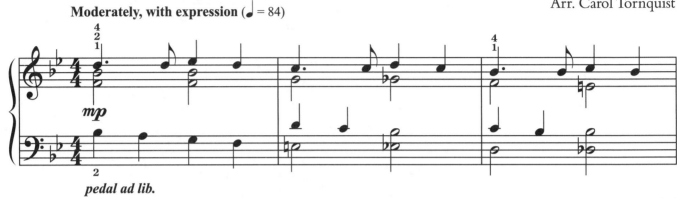

14

(Approx. Performance Time – 2:30)

THE LONGER I SERVE HIM

Words and Music by William J. Gaither
Arr. Carol Tornquist

(Approx. Performance Time – 2:45)

THE FAMILY OF GOD
WITH
JESUS, WE JUST WANT TO THANK YOU

"The Family of God"
Words by William J. and Gloria Gaither
Music by William J. Gaither

Arr. Carol Tornquist

Flowing ($\quad$ = 92)

"Jesus, We Just Want to Thank You"
Words by William J. and Gloria Gaither
Music by William J. Gaither

20

"The Family of God"

(Approx. Performance Time – 2:45)

COME, HOLY SPIRIT

Words by William J. and Gloria Gaither
Music by William J. Gaither
Arr. Carol Tornquist

Moderately, with expression (♩ = 92)

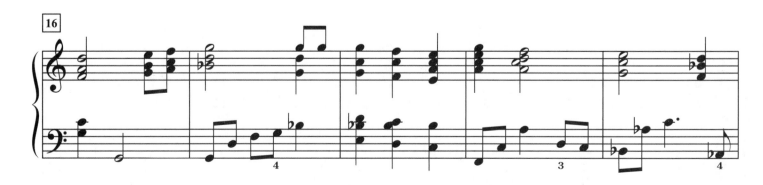

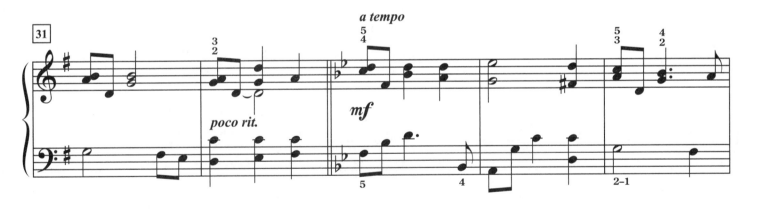

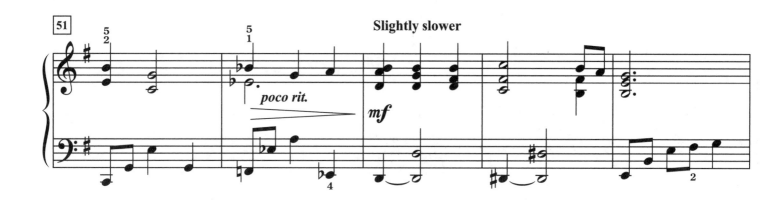

(Approx. Performance Time – 2:45)

THE KING IS COMING

Words by William J. and Gloria Gaither and Charles Millhuff
Music by William J. Gaither
Arr. Carol Tornquist

(Approx. Performance Time – 3:45)

GENTLE SHEPHERD

Words by Gloria Gaither
Music by William J. Gaither
Arr. Carol Tornquist

Slowly, with expression (♩ = 84)

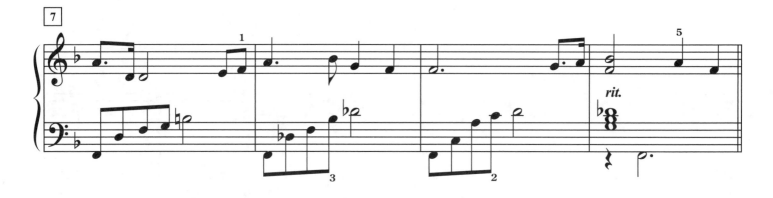

(Approx. Performance Time – 2:15)

Jesus Is Lord of All

Words by William J. and Gloria Gaither
Music by William J. Gaither
Arr. Carol Tornquist

Moderately, with expression (♩ = 88)

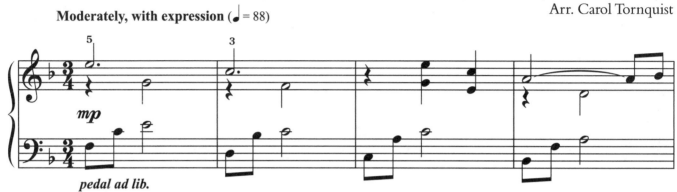

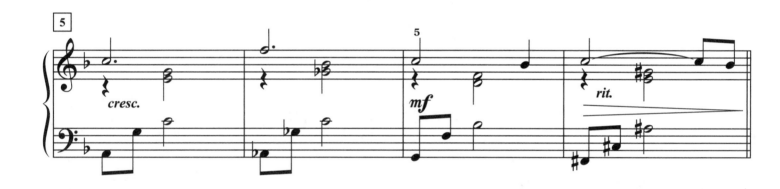

(Approx. Performance Time – 2:15)

I Will Serve Thee

Words by William J. and Gloria Gaither
Music by William J. Gaither
Arr. Carol Tornquist

HE TOUCHED ME

Verse 1:

Shackled by a heavy burden,
'Neath a load of guilt and shame;
Then the hand of Jesus touched me,
And now I am no longer the same.

Chorus:

He touched me,
Oh, He touched me,
And oh, the joy that floods my soul!
Something happened and now I know,
He touched me and made me whole.

Verse 2:

Since I met this blessed Savior,
Since He cleansed and made me whole,
I will never cease to praise Him—
I'll shout it while eternity rolls.

Chorus

SOMETHING BEAUTIFUL

Something beautiful, something good;
All my confusion He understood.
All I had to offer Him was brokenness and strife,
But He made something beautiful of my life.

If there ever were dreams that were lofty and noble,
They were my dreams at the start.
And the hopes for life's best were the hopes that I harbored
Down deep in my heart.
But my dreams turned to ashes,
My castles all crumbled,
My fortune turned to loss.
So I wrapped it all in the rags of my life,
And laid it at the cross!

Something beautiful, something good;
All my confusion He understood.
All I had to offer Him was brokenness and strife,
But He made something beautiful of my life.

THERE'S SOMETHING ABOUT THAT NAME

Chorus:

Jesus, Jesus, Jesus;
There's just something about that name.
Master, Savior, Jesus,
Like the fragrance after the rain.
Jesus, Jesus, Jesus,
Let all Heaven and earth proclaim;
Kings and kingdoms will all pass away,
But there's something about that name.

Recitation 1:

*Jesus, the mere mention of His Name can calm the storm,
heal the broken, raise the dead. At the Name of Jesus, I've seen
sin-hardened men melted, derelicts transformed, the lights of hope put
back into the eyes of a hopeless child…*

*At the Name of Jesus, hatred and bitterness turned to love and
forgiveness, arguments cease.*

*I've heard a mother softly breathe His Name at the bedside of
a child delirious from fever, and I've watched that little body grow
quiet and the fevered brow cool.*

*I've sat beside a dying saint, her body racked with pain, who
in those final fleeting seconds summoned her last ounce of ebbing
strength to whisper earth's sweetest Name—*

Chorus

Recitation 2:

*Emperors have tried to destroy it; philosophies have tried to
stamp it out. Tyrants have tried to wash it from the face of the earth
with the very blood of those who claimed it. Yet still it stands.*

*And there shall be that final day when every voice that has
ever uttered a sound—every voice of Adam's race shall raise in one
great mighty chorus to proclaim the Name of Jesus—for in that day
"Every knee shall bow and every tongue shall confess that Jesus Christ
is Lord!!!"*

*Ah—so you see—it was not mere chance that caused the
angel one night long ago to say to a virgin maiden, "His Name shall
be called Jesus."*

Chorus

BECAUSE HE LIVES

Verse 1:
God sent His Son, they called him Jesus;
He came to love, heal and forgive;
He lived and died to buy my pardon,
An empty grave is there to prove my Savior lives.

Chorus:
Because He lives I can face tomorrow;
Because He lives all fear is gone;
Because I know He holds the future,
And life is worth the living just because He lives!

Verse 2:
How sweet to hold a newborn baby,
And feel the pride and joy He gives;
But greater still the calm assurance,
This child can face uncertain days because He lives.

Chorus

Verse 3:

And then one day I'll cross that river;
I'll fight life's final war with pain;
And then as death gives way to vict'ry,
I'll see the lights of glory and I'll know He reigns.

Chorus

THE LONGER I SERVE HIM

Verse 1:
Since I started for the Kingdom,
Since my life He controls,
Since I gave my heart to Jesus,
The longer I serve Him, the sweeter He grows.

Chorus:
The longer I serve Him, the sweeter He grows,
The more that I love Him, more love He bestows.
Each day is like heaven, my heart overflows,
The longer I serve Him, the sweeter He grows.

Verse 2:
Ev'ry need He is supplying,
Plenteous grace He bestows;
Ev'ry day my way gets brighter,
The longer I serve Him, the sweeter He grows.

Chorus

THE FAMILY OF GOD

Chorus:
I'm so glad I'm a part of the fam'ly of God!
I've been washed in the fountain,
Cleansed by His blood.
Joint heirs with Jesus as we travel this sod,
For I'm part of the fam'ly, the fam'ly of God.

Verse 1:
You will notice we say brother and sister 'round here,
It's because we're a fam'ly and these folks are so near.
When one has a heartache we all share the tears,
And rejoice in each vict'ry in this fam'ly so dear.

Chorus

Verse 2:
From the door of an orph'nage to the house of the King,
No longer an outcast, a new song I sing.
From rags unto riches from the weak to the strong,
I'm not worthy to be here, but, praise God, I belong!

Chorus

JESUS, WE JUST WANT TO THANK YOU

Verse 1:
Jesus, we just want to thank You,
Jesus, we just want to thank You,
Jesus, we just want to thank You,
Thank You for being so good.

Verse 2:
Jesus, we just want to praise You,
Jesus, we just want to praise You,
Jesus, we just want to praise You,
Praise You for being so good.

Verse 3:
Jesus, we just want to tell You,
Jesus, we just want to tell You,
Jesus, we just want to tell You,
We love You for being so good.

Verse 4:
Savior, we just want to serve You,
Savior, we just want to serve You,
Savior, we just want to serve You,
Serve You for being so good.

Verse 5:
Jesus, we know You are coming,
Jesus, we know You are coming,
Jesus, we know You are coming,
Take us to live in Your home.

COME, HOLY SPIRIT

Verse 1:
Come as a wisdom to children,
Come as new sight to the blind,
Come, Lord, as strength to my weakness,
Take me: soul, body and mind.

Chorus:
Come, Holy Spirit, I need You,
Come, sweet Spirit, I pray;
Come in Your strength and Your power,
Come in Your own gentle way.

Verse 2:
Come as a rest to the weary,
Come as a balm for the sore,
Come as a dew to my dryness;
Fill me with joy evermore.

Chorus

Verse 3:
Come like a spring in the desert,
Come to the withered of soul;
O let Your sweet healing power
Touch me and make me whole.

Chorus

THE KING IS COMING

The market place is empty,
No more traffic in the streets,
All the builders' tools are silent,
No more time to harvest wheat;
Busy housewives cease their labors,
In the courtroom no debate,
Work on earth is all suspended
As the King comes thro' the gate.

Happy faces line the hallways,
Those whose lives have been redeemed,
Broken homes that He has mended,
Those from prison He has freed;
Little children and the aged
Hand-in-hand stand all aglow,
Who were crippled, broken, ruined,
Clad in garments white as snow.

I can hear the chariots rumble,
I can see that marching throng,
The flurry of God's trumpets
Spell the end of sin and wrong;
Regal robes are now unfolding,
Heaven's grandstands all in place,
Heaven's choir is now assembled,
Start to sing Amazing Grace!

Oh, the King is coming! The King is coming!
I just heard the trumpet sounding and now His face I see;
Oh, the King is coming! The King is coming!
Praise God, He's coming for me!

Oh, the King is coming! The King is coming!
I just heard the trumpet sounding and now His face I see;
Oh, the King is coming! The King is coming!
Praise God, He's coming for me!

GENTLE SHEPHERD

Gentle Shepherd, come and lead us,
For we need You to help us find our way.
Gentle Shepherd, come and feed us,
For we need Your strength from day to day.
There's no other we can turn to
Who can help us face another day;
Gentle Shepherd, come and lead us,
For we need You to help us find our way.

JESUS IS LORD OF ALL

Verse 1:
All my tomorrows, all my past,
Jesus is Lord of all.
I've quit my struggles, contentment at last.
Jesus is Lord of all.

Chorus:
King of kings, Lord of lords,
Jesus is Lord of all.
All my possessions and all my life,
Jesus is Lord of all.

Verse 2:
All of my conflicts, all my thoughts,
Jesus is Lord of all.
His love wins the battles I could not have fought.
Jesus is Lord of all.

Chorus

Verse 3:
All of my longings, all my dreams,
Jesus is Lord of all.
All of my failures His power redeems.
Jesus is Lord of all.

Chorus

I WILL SERVE THEE

I will serve Thee because I love Thee;
You have given life to me.
I was nothing before You found me;
You have given life to me.

Heartaches, broken pieces,
Ruined lives are why You died on Calv'ry.
Your touch was what I longed for;
You have given life to me.